The Bamboo Oracle

The Bamboo Oracle

Confucian Wisdom for Every Day

Chao-Hsiu Chen

JOURNEY EDITIONS
BOSTON • TOKYO

First published in the United States in 1998 by Journey Editions,
an imprint of Periplus Editions (HK) Ltd., with editorial offices at
153 Milk Street, Boston, Massachussetts 02109.

Library of Congress Catalog Card Number: 98–86147

ISBN 1-885203-67-5

Distributed by

North America	Japan	Southeast Asia
Charles E. Tuttle Co., Inc.	Tuttle Shokai Ltd.	Berkeley Books Pte. Ltd.
RR1 Box 231-5	1–21–13, Seki	5 Little Road #08–01
North Clarendon	Tama-Ku, Kawasaki-shi	Singapore 536983
VT 05759	Kanagawa-ken 214, Japan	Tel: (65) 280-3320
Tel: (802) 773-8930	Tel: (044) 833-0225	Fax: (65) 280-6290
Tel: (800) 526-2778	Fax: (044) 822-0413	

First Edition
06 05 04 03 02 01 00 99 98   1 3 5 7 9 10 8 6 4 2

AN EDDISON • SADD EDITION
Edited, designed and produced by
Eddison Sadd Editions Limited
St Chad's House, 148 King Cross Road
London WC1X 9DH

Phototypeset in Bernhard Modern using QuarkXPress on Apple Macintosh
Origination by Bright Arts PTE Ltd., Singapore
Printed and bound by Sheck Wah Tong Printing Press Ltd., Hong Kong
Packed by Hung Hing, China

Contents

Introduction

The possibilities of using bamboo are manifold. Not only is it a popular plant around the world, but out of its wood we produce a vast range of items, from chopsticks, flutes, cups and vases, to broomhandles, beach mats, Venetian blinds and furniture; even water-pipe systems and houses can be built from bamboo. The young bamboo shoots are appreciated as a delicacy all over the world, and without its leaves many Asian meals would not exist. Bamboo, therefore, plays an important role in the material world.

However, little known in the West is that bamboo also possesses a special spiritual power originating from its very nature (see 'Speaks the Bamboo' on page 8). Those of us who have ever had the chance to walk in a bamboo wood, with trees as high as forty metres (only in the West do we know bamboo as a bush), and those of us who have been touched by the sunlight breaking the tender foliage, know how easily this tree can enchant the human soul. Even painting bamboo is meditation: there are Chinese artists who paint nothing but bamboo all their lives. To Asian peoples, bamboo has always been a symbol for a spiritual realm which finds its counterpart in the secular order. Confucius, perhaps the most famous of all Far Eastern Wise Men, translated this realm to earthly life, in order that this should lead to a just and righteous world and, thus, a fulfilled life.

Confucius was born on 21 October in the year 551 BC, in the principality of Lu on the peninsula Shantung ('Mount of the East'). At the age of fifteen he began to study the classic Chinese writings, to follow their precepts and, moreover, to teach these precepts to others. During his lifetime he is said to have taught over three thousand students. In 515 BC, the famous meeting with Lao Tzu (the legendary founder of Taoism) took place; Confucius left this meeting enthusiastically. Aged sixty-eight, he began to compose all those writings that distinguish him as a wise and just thinker, writings that even to this day constitute a fundamental part of Chinese literature.

Confucius died on 11 April 478 BC; his 'doctrine', however, was not made official until 399 years after his death. A contemporary of Buddha, Confucius worked on giving a basis to the Chinese culture – not by founding a religion but by appealing to us all to find our way back to our 'selves' in order to regain harmony with ourselves, the people around us and nature as a whole. It is no accident that it is said in *Lun Yu*, the 'Book of Conversations':

'I am looking for a saint and do not find him; if I were able to find a noble person, much would be gained. I am looking out for a good person, but do not own him; if I were able to find a persistent person, that would be worth much. Keeping up appearances, as if owning something; being empty and simulating abundance; being in great difficulties and pretending to live in rich peace: being indeed persistent in this is difficult.'

It is my aim to introduce to the West the Chinese art of ennobling the character and living a happy life on the basis of Confucian wisdom. Particularly in our age of disorientation, with so many questions being asked on the meaning of existence, it seems necessary to me to offer help to all advice-seekers through the magic of the bamboo and the content of the Confucian teaching. This is why I have developed this oracle system, which I hope will give the right answers to whoever is asking. It allows us all to access these teachings, using the sixty-four hexagrams of the *I Ching* as its basis. By choosing six bamboo cards, and then selecting one of the bamboo sticks if you require deeper insight, you are able to create hexagrams which offer guidance in answer to your question *(see 'How to Use the Oracle' on pages 9–12)*. For each hexagram, I have written a poem to express its traditional meaning, as well as an interpretation of this meaning for your life; you will find these included on pages 13–141.

But first let us listen to what the bamboo wants to tell us …

Speaks the Bamboo

From time immemorial I have been regarded as a symbol for the noble character of man. Neither by flowers nor by fruit do I seek to touch others; I do not bribe or persuade. I am how I am: silent, modest, deeply rooted.

Even if the wind masses all its forces together, it is only able to bend me; it cannot break me because my joints are too strong. They resemble the respectability and the just feeling of virtue.

Inside, I have no burden and am full of frankness and emptiness, humility and modesty. To this emptiness corresponds, as Lao Tzu says, the abundance. Because only an empty heart is always ready to learn – and everything that lives inside is contributing to the abundance of the soul.

'Without food you lose power, without bamboo grace' wrote the poet Su Tung Po, who was full of good-heartedness. But to become this noble character, you have to go a long way. It is also necessary to recognize which talents to foster and which talents to let rest. These talents are only the key to wisdom that already lies within you. And only you are able to guide them out of the darkness of sleep into the light of alertness. If I may serve you as an example, you will soon succeed ...

Why do we live?
To accumulate knowledge,
to acquire skills?
I do not take care neither
for the one nor for the other
and recall my roots.
That is my duty.
That is my way.
That is why I live.
I try to understand my roots.
Because this knowledge makes me grow.
And my heart is full and empty at the same time.
So I can be happy.

How to Use the Oracle

The oracle is easy to use, even for those without any prior experience or knowledge of Chinese philosophy. It consists of sixty-four cards, each one depicting a unique Chinese bamboo painting, twelve bamboo divining sticks, and interpretational texts, which are included in this book. When you have asked your question, you should not read the text as a direct answer, but rather you should interpret it as guidance on how you could change your situation.

The system for accessing the readings derives from the Chinese oracle of the *I Ching*, or 'Book of Changes'. This ancient book of fortune was written about 5000 years ago and is based on the polarity of all things, which consist of *yin* (the female element identified by the symbol ▬ ▬) and *yang* (the male element identified by the symbol ▬▬▬). If yin and yang lines are combined into groups of three (which are known as trigrams) there are eight possible variations. When these eight trigrams are placed vertically in pairs, the sixty-four six-line 'sayings' (hexagrams) originate, forming the basis for the questioning of the oracle.

The bamboo cards each have a yin or yang line printed on the reverse side – there are thirty-two yin cards and thirty-two yang cards – and these lines allow you to build a hexagram. The back of each card also carries a number from 1 to 64: these numbers are only used when you consult the oracle using the bamboo sticks.

Using the Cards

Make sure you always handle the cards carefully and with respect; your relationship with them will have a direct bearing on the accuracy of the message you will receive from your chosen hexagram. Whenever you wish to consult the oracle there is a series of steps that you must follow, and these stages are outlined below.

1. PREPARE
Lay the cards down in front of you on a large flat surface, with the bamboo side facing upwards. It does not matter if the cards overlap a little. Close your eyes and focus your mind on your question.

2. SHUFFLE

Now open your eyes and stir the cards by moving them around – still face up – on the surface. As you do this, contemplate them as they pass across your gaze. Let the subtle energies and influences of the bamboo images interact with your subconscious.

3. SELECT

During this process, respond to the feeling that you are drawn to a particular card, whether by its colour or by its design, and place the card to one side, face up. Draw five more cards in this way, placing them face up on top of the first card so that you end up with a pile of six cards.

4. READ

Turn the pile over, so that the cards are face down. You can now read the yin or yang line on the back. Draw the first line on a piece of paper, then draw the line from the second card above it and the line from the third card above that, continuing through all six cards until you have completed your hexagram, building from bottom to top.

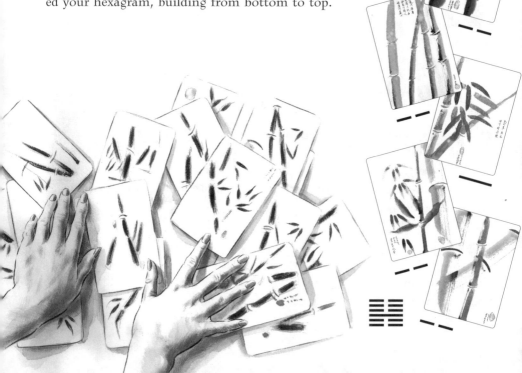

5. CONSULT

Now find your hexagram in the index on page 144. Once you are sure that it matches exactly, note its number and name, turn to the correct page and read the wisdom that is offered for this moment in your life. The poem expresses the traditional meaning of the hexagram, and the text offers an interpretation of this meaning as guidance for your life.

Using the Bamboo Sticks

If you find that you still need deeper insight and guidance after having consulted the cards, you can turn to the bamboo sticks. Each of these carries a number from 1 to 12. Hold the sticks in your hand, making sure the numbers are at the bottom so that they are concealed. Hold your hand in front of your forehead (your 'Third Eye'), and once again focus on your question in a meditative way. Select one of the sticks and follow the card shuffle and selection procedure indicated by its number (see list overleaf). This leads you to two further hexagrams, which offer guidance from a mental and practical perspective.

For example, if you draw bamboo stick 6, you would shuffle the cards (having replaced the six previously drawn cards back in the pack) and pick out four cards that you are drawn to, placing them face up in a pile. You then reshuffle the remaining cards, and pick out a further two, adding them to the top of the pile. Turn the cards over and, as before, compile a hexagram using the yin and yang lines on the back. This hexagram offers guidance from a mental 'How should I think about this issue?' perspective. For a practical 'What action should I take?' perspective, you need to consult your keycard. This is always the last card of the first group selected – so for bamboo stick 6, the keycard is the fourth one. Note the number printed on the back of the card and then refer to the relevant hexagram for guidance.

SELECTION PROCEDURE

BAMBOO STICK 1
- Shuffle and pick up one.
- Shuffle and pick up one.
- Shuffle and pick up one.
- Shuffle and pick up one.
- Shuffle and pick up one.
- Shuffle and pick up one.

Keycard: the first card.

BAMBOO STICK 2
- Shuffle and pick up three.
- Shuffle and pick up three.

Keycard: the third card.

BAMBOO STICK 3
- Shuffle and pick up six.

Keycard: the sixth card.

BAMBOO STICK 4
- Shuffle and pick up two.
- Shuffle and pick up two.
- Shuffle and pick up two.

Keycard: the second card.

BAMBOO STICK 5
- Shuffle and pick up two.
- Shuffle and pick up four.

Keycard: the second card.

BAMBOO STICK 6
- Shuffle and pick up four.
- Shuffle and pick up two.

Keycard: the fourth card.

BAMBOO STICK 7
- Shuffle and pick up five.
- Shuffle and pick up one.

Keycard: the fifth card.

BAMBOO STICK 8
- Shuffle and pick up one.
- Shuffle and pick up five.

Keycard: the first card.

BAMBOO STICK 9
- Shuffle and pick up one.
- Shuffle and pick up two.
- Shuffle and pick up three.

Keycard: the first card.

BAMBOO STICK 10
- Shuffle and pick up three.
- Shuffle and pick up two.
- Shuffle and pick up one.

Keycard: the third card.

BAMBOO STICK 11
- Shuffle and pick up two.
- Shuffle and pick up one.
- Shuffle and pick up three.

Keycard: the second card.

BAMBOO STICK 12
- Shuffle and pick up two.
- Shuffle and pick up three.
- Shuffle and pick up one.

Keycard: the second card.

THE ORACLE

C H I E N

1

*Self-control
requires practical knowledge.
Self-knowledge
requires a reasonable view.*

Now you have come to a moment in your life when you must make a far-sighted decision. If you do not know how to handle it, then it is necessary to pause for a while. In the meantime, contemplate the achievements you have made to this day and think back to the time before you made them. This is how you will reach a reasonable view which will help you to solve the problem. But do not forget that the real understanding of yourself is more important than the decision itself.

K'UN

2

Humility and modesty
are the best protection
against the wrong opinion
of others.

With a peaceful heart
things happen
by themselves.

He who rests in himself
is not acquainted with enemies.

Neither fame nor richness
set the heart in motion.

The less emotively you try to deal with your problem, the calmer your soul will become. Everything acts of its own accord. Nobody forces you to react. Imagine what would happen if you did not exist; how would events develop? You will soon recognize that a negative event is able to bring forth a positive result.

䷂ C H U N

3

Whenever you try to be the first
there will be one to thrust you aside.
Whatever you want to reach at first
will always be reached by somebody else.
As this is one of earth's laws
try to stay calm
and you will reach the goal – without noticing it.

You have lost your way. But if you remember the fable of the tortoise and the rabbit, then you will see that the first is not always the first, and that even the last can be the first. It seems that there is a secret power by which we are all led. This power will show you your final destination, even if you are not able to recognize it yourself. Yet your fortune is in your hands, because your ideas and actions change the world by each day, by each hour, by each minute, by each second. It is necessary, however, always to remain cautious.

M E N G

4

You only reach self-control
if you pay homage to solicitude
as well in speaking as in doing.

If you grant the solicitude
enough space in your heart
then you will find the fullness of the void.

Everything you do should be handled with care. Try to look at all things as living beings, rather than simply as useful objects or items. Whatever exists in this world contains atoms – and atoms are 'alive'; therefore even a chair can be regarded as a living being. For that reason it is necessary to treat human beings with respect and understanding. The more you give, the more you will have.

H
S
U

5

*Each misery
is the result
of intolerance.*

You should learn to wait. Impatience never yields success. The solution always appears suddenly and from an unexpected direction. And there is always a solution. If you cannot find one, let yourself be found *by* the solution.

䷅ SUNG

6

Good events
will fade away.
Bad events
will fade away.
Too much pleasure
will cause damage to the soul.
Too much sorrow
will cause damage to the heart.

Eternal change is nature's way. It is wise not to feel either too much joy or too much sorrow. Everything fades away, everything comes again. The best way to bear the constant changing is to find the peace in your heart. What makes you happy today can make you sad tomorrow. What brings you sadness today might bring you happiness tomorrow.

S H I H

7

Fill up your heart with emptiness,
your body with virtue.
Encounter all living beings with goodness
and bend your head with respect
in the face of life.

None of us can avoid the changing of life, nor elevate ourselves above it; but we can resist the different temptations. Adjust your inner view from now on: be full of courage and trust the power which enables you to live.

☷ P

I

8

He who remains
unimpressed by the outward appearance
will find silence within.

He who does not know
fear any longer
will find that there is no outward appearance.

All that surrounds us is an illusion. Reality is dependent on our own imagination. If you are afraid of something, you fear only the image you have formed from a subject, a person or a situation. Destroy this image and break through to the essence.

H S I A O C H'U

9

Do not be downhearted when you are alone;
be helpful when you are with people;
be clear in mind when nothing is happening;
be brave with your decision when there is
*   confusion;*
be modest when you are successful;
be silent when the success leaves you slowly
*   behind.*

Success can never be permanent: it comes as quickly it goes. But there is one success which remains forever – you can find it in practising the art of sharing. If you do not claim the success only for yourself, but let others share it as well, then you find the secret of success. The law of success relates to life as a whole.

 L
U

10

You are not discreet enough
but do not cause any damage;
you make a wrong decision
but you achieve success;
you cannot control yourself
but you desire profit;
therefore you think this is normal
and you cannot recognize the right behaviour
    any longer.
From this moment on there is a danger
you may cause real damage to yourself and to
    others.

Ask yourself what success really means to you. Ask yourself whether you really should believe the adulation paid to you by others. Look within yourself and reflect on both the advantages and disadvantages of your thoughts and ideas. If you discover that your actions are likely to harm someone, stop at once – even if you feel that you may lose out. Only then can you find the real benefit.

䷊ T'
A
I

11

If you learn to go a step backwards
then you reach a step forwards.
Even if you were to own great treasures
it would not make you happier —
unless you are able
to invest it only for the greatest good.

Nothing ends in itself. Everything has a special
sense. The difficulty is how to recognize this sense,
because it is likely only to become apparent after
the event has taken place. You should, therefore,
aim all your deeds and actions towards the gen-
eral good, in order that others may become as
lucky as you hope to be yourself.

P'I

12

Who does not esteem oneself
does not deserve to be treasured.
Who does not handle the deeds with care
will cause damage.
Who does not esteem others
does not deserve to be treasured.

Even if you handle everything with a great deal of care, it is still not enough. Even if love accompanies the care, it is not yet enough. Only if respect is the companion of care and love will you be able to estimate everything according to the right degree.

T'UNG JEN

13

The more one reduces the wishes
the purer the heart will become.

The more courteous the behaviour
the more respectable is the character.

Whatever you do not own you cannot lose. Whatever you do not desire, you do not have to reach. The less you require for yourself and from others, the clearer your mind and the purer your heart will be. Intentions always lead to pressure. Always consider that everything has its own life to lead.

T

A

Y

U

14

If you have done enough stop your work.
If you have spoken enough keep silent.
Every mistake is a violation against time.
A noble character does not need to draw attention.

All that happens will end in the borders of time. Happiness is composed of meeting the right person at the right place, in the right moment. But these events do not happen by chance: they are led by an inner necessity. You yourself are the one who is able to create an event such as this — together with the others who are involved. The more understated your appearance, the less fear you have to have.

C H' I E N

15

Greatest peace
in
modesty.

Greatest modesty
in
silence.

Yesterday you wished to have something, today you have changed your mind already – and what will it be tomorrow? You are not able to make a decision and you always lay the blame on others. Do not become a slave of your wishes. Is it not better that they remain within your control? Only if you are independent from wishes and from suffering will you find your inner self.

Y
U

16

Slow down your thoughts.
Moderate your body's requirements.
Keep your tongue behind your teeth.
Choose the right friends in order to grow.
Explore your behaviour in order to mature.
If you think you are noble
be the best critic of yourself.

How often have you looked at yourself in the mirror? And what have you seen? Your outer appearance. But which mirror reveals your deep, inner self? The right friends. And who are the right friends? Those who criticize you. What happens if you do not have them? Then be the best friend of yourself.

S U I

17

Forgive the mistakes of others – full of love.
Measure the deeds of yourself – with care.
Forgive the mistakes of yourself – with care.
Measure the deeds of others – full of love.

Before you criticize others, criticize yourself. Before you forgive yourself, forgive others. And do so full of respect and love. If this is not the case, then your deeds are similar to those between two enemies. And life is too short to have enemies.

KU

18

*Be patient
in all situations.
Be steady
in every matter.*

Everything that happens does so because of its own dynamic. It is better to follow the energetic field of this dynamic instead of fighting against it. Only if you are in harmony with each happening will you develop the greatness and the power necessary to enfold your inner strength.

L I N

19

If you go onwards
your radius will contract.
If you look backwards
your radius will enlarge.

You are the result of all your prevailing deeds, thoughts, ideas, pleasures and sorrows. If you seek luck in the future, you will be disappointed. Only at this moment – right now and right here – can you be completely in your presence. Keep your focus in the present, but do not let the future and the past stray out of your sight.

KUAN

20

If you are surrounded by others
and still able
to find your own way
then you have
a clear sight.

If fate troubles you
and you are still able
to lead a steady life
then you have
very deep roots.

An opinion is only an opinion *about* an opinion. Do not let yourself be influenced too much. Find your own way: this does not have to be the road in front of you – you also can take a side road. If you still believe in yourself then you know the direction of your way, even if you find yourself at a crossroads.

☲☳ S
H
I
H HO

21

If the facts change
from one moment to another
it is better to keep quiet
instead of giving up too quickly.
Even if you do not see any chance
to avoid the complication
you know that you are on the right path
and your heart remains innocent.

No event leads only to negative results; a negative outcome is only considered if it affects your personal interests. Everything always has two sides. Therefore that which seems bad today can become good tomorrow. You need to keep your mind clear and make sure you do not hurt others – even if you cannot find any way out of the situation. By doing this you help others as well as yourself, and suddenly a new, unexpected path will appear in front of you.

P
I

22

Serious be your endeavour
joyful your attention.
Liberal be your generosity
careful your desire.

All wishes are born out of either necessity or insolence. Therefore, most remain unfulfilled and will be replaced by new wishes which will have the same fate. If you treat your wishes just as you want to be treated by others yourself, you can be sure that they will be achieved.

䷖ PO

23

There are people
whom you will never meet.
But there are questions
you cannot avoid.
There are people
whom you will never meet.
But there are answers
you cannot escape.

Only by respecting yourself and others are you able to bear any kind of question; and only in this frame of mind can you stand the answers. If you meet the right person you will get the right answer; if you meet the wrong person, wrong questions will be asked.

䷗ F
U

24

Think widely
but do not forget
the exactness.
Act conscientiously
but do not forget
the indulgence.

At the moment you find yourself in a mood which requires cautious action. You should learn how to forgive if you want to reach your goals. Not everything must be realized according to your wish. Other people have the same rights. You must be ready to compromise. Do not think only straight ahead; think in other directions, too.

WU WANG

25

Train your impartiality
and close your ears in the face of defamation.
Train your moderation
and bend your head in the face of humiliation.

You have no enemies. The only enemy you have is yourself. If you try to understand the cause behind the problem, you will notice that your 'enemies' are as weak as yourself. Rivalry only leads to damage and pain. Learn to fight without winning.

T
A
C
H'
U

大
玄
田

26

Not everything has to be done.
Not everything has to be said.
The most beautiful moment is
when the flower is in half-bloom.

Whatever you want to know, do not forget that each thought creates a new question. Stop asking questions and be assured that everything will be good if you trust in yourself.

I

27

Only he who is not worthy
of fame
fights for it.

He who is worthy of it
will meet it while asleep.

There is no sense in reaching a goal through violence. If the goal wishes, it will come to you. Stay modest, therefore, and do not forget that true success is to make others lucky.

T A
K
U O

28

The more confusing a situation is
the less one should think about it.
The more incomprehensible a person is
the warmer one should deal with him.
The quicker a matter is
the slower one should handle it.
This is the secret of being strong without
  strength.

You should find the quietness in yourself. Only from within can you develop the power that you need in order to bear life's problems. Do not insist on your position – do not fight; be fearless, and you will be able to face all the negative happenings and change them into positive ones.

䷜K' A N

29

The will of a single person seldom has success
if it is against the multitude.
To be against the will of the multitude
never has success.
Although the will of the multitude is not able
to break the will of a single person.

If you are weak in certain situations then this
does not mean that you have to give up your
principles. Even if it seems that your principles
contradict those of others, you will reach your
goal – but only if you try to do so without ego-
tism. All your ideas will be successfully realized
if you understand who you, yourself, can be.

☲ LI

30

Pretending to know
what you do not really know
does not prove any intelligence.

Pretending that something happens
although nothing happens
does not prove any fulfilment.

Pretending being able to realize
what you are not really able to
does not prove any power of your spirit.

Therefore choose what you do not want to do.

It does not mean that you are weak if you are
unable to handle certain situations. Show your
weakness. Nobody will judge you. Present yourself as a human being who is thankful for each
suggestion. We can all only learn from one other,
and each of us knows something which another
does not know.

H
S
I
E
N

31

If there is nothing to do
it is good to avoid distraction.
If there is much to do
it is good to sink into your inner self.

Life has prepared many 'requirements' of you. Would you like to be its slave? Or would you prefer to settle the requirements yourself? If so, withdraw into yourself and try to solve the problems from within. The root cause of a problem will not relate to its outer appearance.

HENG

32

If you do not know
how to handle a matter
then this means
that the heart is not educated enough.

One only educates the heart
if one leaves it to the void.

One can educate the heart
but not the matter.

If the heart is educated
one can deal
with every matter.

You can bear each situation and solve each problem if it is clear that you are the one who has to do something. Never forget that only the heart is able to make either something good or something bad out of everything. It just depends on how much you trust your heart.

THE ORACLE

TUN

33

*To solve problems
one needs quietness.
If one is in a hurry
one has enough to
deal with oneself.
How can one possibly still have
time to solve problems?*

How can you be of use if you are now full of anger, agitation or despair? Meditate and think about what this anger, this agitation or this despair could bring you. Is it not better to keep your distance from the problems without giving up your responsibility?

T A   C H U A N G

34

Do not make promises
when you are full of joy.
Do not make promises
when you are full of sorrow.

Make your promises only when you are level-
headed and calm. Think without emotions, then
your decisions will always be right.

䷢ C H I N

35

If one tries
to imitate you
it is wiser
to bear it
instead of to defend yourself.

If one tries
to criticize you
it is wiser
to bear it
instead of to raise yourself above it.

When negative things happen to you, treat them
as a learning process. Nothing and no one is
really against you; if they were, you would not
even be on this earth to begin with. Had you
not been chosen, you would not be here now.
Each criticism, each reprimand, therefore, can
only strengthen you.

䷣ MING I

明夷

36

To overcome a complication
you should overcome your anger
and replace it
with your inner power.

To pacify a complicated person
you should overcome your anger
and replace it
with understanding.

Inner power and understanding are the precon-
ditions for a happy life. If you avoid the anger,
others will admire you for this. They will prob-
ably even follow your example.

C
H
I
A

J
E
N

37

If you meet someone
who could understand you
and you do not speak to him
then you have lost the chance.

If you meet someone
who could not understand you
and you do speak to him
then you have lost your words.

All difficulties arise from a wrong communication. It is necessary, therefore, to learn how to listen to and how to understand others. Only those who are able to listen will be able to understand.

K'UEI

38

You have taken over responsibility
but if you take it too lightly
there will be repercussions
even if you try to repair it later on.

You have taken over responsibility
and if you take it seriously
you will receive compliments
even if you become more easy-going later on.

First you should strengthen your full understanding of the situation; afterwards, you should nurture your ability to let go. Then people will feel grateful for what you have done, and everybody will achieve what they want to achieve. If you do things the other way round, you will not reach your goal.

C
H
I
E
N

39

The one who knows how to use their own power
does not show off.
The one who knows how to use their own goodness
does not show it often.
The one who knows their own effect
avoids spectators.
The one who knows how to keep promises
makes it with care.

Be discreet whenever the situation requires it. Wait, and try to avoid boasting. It is very easy to shout and to call the attention of the public to you, but it will not last long. If you want to be respected all the time, it is necessary to be cautious.

H
S
I
E
H

40

If you want to make someone
notice their own mistake
it is not wise
to talk about it immediately.
It is better to praise their virtues first.

You should not heed this advice as a clever trick by which you are able to achieve your goals, but rather as a way of showing respect to others, because no one makes mistakes on purpose. In addition, you will be able to help the other person to understand and correct the mistake without causing any embarrassment.

䷒ SUN

41

To give good influence to someone
it is important
to begin the matter seriously
but with a very friendly tone
and very thoughtful words.
Face the facts of the inadequacy,
forgive the deficiencies,
notice the lack of knowledge
and be not in opposition to the wishes.

To give good influence to someone
it is important
to find the right place
and the right timing,
the right behaviour and the right mood,
even the right gestures.
After all of this someone will be able
to give good influence – to you.

All things relate to – and depend on – all other things. The only thing that we can actively do is to help ourselves to make decisions more easily by following the advice given above.

I

42

*If you notice that someone wants to betray you
pretend that you do not know it.
If you notice that someone wants to offend you
pretend that you do not know it.
If you notice that someone wants to praise you
pretend that you do not know it.
If you notice that someone wants to adore you
pretend that you do not know it.*

A real master of life acts with silence, whatever
may happen. This is how they make others mas-
ters of life as well.

KUAI

43

*The most important thing
to help a child grow
is the purity of heart.*

*The most important thing
to help a family grow
is the togetherness of hearts.*

*The most important thing
to help a society grow
is the peace of hearts.*

Hate and envy will never create something steady.
Jealousy and greed will cause people to stay away
from you. Try to overcome your ego and respond
to others.

KOU

44

*Always think of the welfare of others
whatever may happen.
Always think of the welfare of others
even if your own prosperity suffers.*

Always put the needs of the ones you love before
your personal interests. In this way you will find
the true fulfilment of your own wishes.

T S' U I

45

A favour
need not be big.
What is important is
that it comes right in time.

A friendship
need not be deep.
What is important is
that it is based on genuine feelings.

The more honestly you treat yourself and others,
the more you will receive the respect you deserve.
Friendships are not created by means of gifts
and presents, but by honest conviction.

䷭ SHENG

46

How is it possible
to avoid being influenced?
Only if you know about your own abilities.

How is it possible
to know your own abilities?
Only if you do not avoid being influenced.

Only then you know who you are.
Only then you know who others are.

To know and understand oneself and others is one of the most difficult goals in life. But the more you immerse yourself in life's adventure, the more you will achieve this ambition. It is necessary only to be always open-minded.

K'
U
N

47

Limited knowledge
brings only discontent.
Limited strength
brings only irritation.
Limited trust
brings only suspicion.
Limited beauty
brings only bragging.

Only if you believe in yourself and your abilities will you lead a life in which you cause others to rejoice. And is there anything more beautiful than to make others happy in this way?

CHING

48

A friendly heart
creates happy people.
A happy heart
creates lucky people.

Do you want your partners to suffer because of you? Or do you want to make them happy? If it is the latter, then try to play down your own problems and instead take care of the sorrows of others. The more you work together with others, the better the world will be.

K
O

49

If you want to suggest something,
the 'how' is more important than the 'what'.
Do not show anything which could awaken greed;
do not show anything which could cause
    disadvantage;
do not show anything which could induce criticism;
do not show anything with severe words;
do not show anything with too many words;
do not show anything with unnecessary words.
Even if your suggestion is good for you it may not
be good for others.

Every opinion is subjective, even if it reflects the truth. This applies both to your own opinions and those of others. If you need to find a solution which satisfies everyone you should take more care of the form than of the contents. And the more pleasant it is, the more others will follow your advice.

TING

50

If there is something unexpected
it is useless to make quick interpretations.
They will only create greater confusion.

Haste overshoots the mark.
The truth approaches it slowly.

Only the right timing can clarify your situation. But how do you know when it is the right time? Trust your inner knowledge and you will be successful.

☷ C
H
E
N

51

To know yourself
is the best way
to know others.

To know others
is the best way
to know the truth.

Whenever there is a problem facing you, in reality this means you have a problem with yourself. You can avoid this if you have learned to listen to yourself and to others, in order to understand them both.

KEN

52

If the outward appearance
triumphs over you, this is because
your inner self
is missing the void.

Only if you are
not self-absorbed
will you be complete in yourself
and find your inner void.

Each kind of menial task leads to selflessness. But it is here that you can find your inner self, because you are not preoccupied with yourself any longer. This moment is one of the most fortuitous in life, but it is only possible to recognize it after it has happened. Do not regret working with seemingly 'senseless' targets. Everything has a sense.

CHIEN

53

If you are accompanied
it is necessary
to mind your words.

If you are alone
it is necessary
to mind your thoughts.

Your words come from your thoughts. It does not matter if you are alone or accompanied: it is important to control your thoughts so that your words cannot cause any harm. All harm that occurs in this world stems from words, and therefore from thoughts. But also, all good things in the world originate from words, and therefore from thoughts.

KUEI MEI

歸
妹

54

He who knows
what will make one content
is not yet content.

He who does not search for something
that will make one content
will be content.

You do not need to spend your life looking for happiness – everything is already there for you. Do not hesitate. Grasp it – but with the right judgement.

FENG

55

Do not be envious of someone else
because of their virtues.
Do not hide your faults
in front of others.
This is the way
you both can grow.

Not to hide your own mistakes, and to accept
your weaknesses, shows how strong you are. If two
people show each other their inner selves, then
something positive will be created throughout
their relationship. This can only be achieved by
meeting people whom you can trust completely.
You can recognize these people by observing that
they do not show off their virtues.

L
U

56

The more beautiful a blossom is
the more seldom it will be discovered.
The more beautiful a word is
The more seldom it is to be heard.

All good things do not display visible effort. This
is why they are so hard to discover. Sharpen your
senses so that you can partake of the beauty. Do
not pay attention to the opinion of the multitude. If you respect the opinion of one person,
you will discover what will be the best for you.

SUN

57

There are abilities
which one can learn.
There are abilities
which one already has.
One is not better than the other.
The only difference is
how one uses them.

The abilities that you were born with, together
with those you have learned through effort, only
make sense if you can use them to help others.

T U I

58

Do not boast
about your
abilities.
Let others
judge
them.

If you do not know
about your
abilities,
let others
help you
to discover them.

Even if you are not successful at the moment, do not stop believing in yourself. You will meet others who will help you to continue on your way. But do not discourage them by boasting too much about yourself.

H U A N

59

The mind of the human being is manifold:
it changes according to the feeling,
the imagination and the happening.
It changes its point of view
whenever it likes
and it always shows a different face
whenever the situation requires it.
But the mind is not separated from you.
It is, with you, in one combined.

Something has happened – and you were expecting the opposite. Do not lose self-control simply because you were unprepared. In reality, you have created this situation yourself. Now you need to be flexible. Only with flexibility you will master the situation.

C H I E H

60

The spirit is alive in your being.
If you want to recognize it
you should look to your roots.

No one is able to withdraw from the attraction of what they could be or what they do not have. You can aspire to these things with pleasure, but never forget where you come from, what you really want and what goal you are really aiming for.

CHUNG FU

中孚

61

Meet people
cordially
and there will be no discord.

Proceed carefully
with matters
and there will be no mistake.

Look open-mindedly
at all happenings
and there will be no fear.

Nourish the soul
with silence
and there will be no greed.

Is it necessary not to live in peace? If you want to live harmoniously, stay silent and listen to the words of your heart.

H
S
I
A
O
#
K
U
O

62

To stop uncertainty
one needs gentleness.

To stop error
one needs visions.

To avoid restlessness
one needs ease.

To abandon inconsideration
one needs tenderness.

To wear down self-praise
one needs understanding.

To stop nagging
one needs generosity.

Learn to be more tolerant, and do not forget that
others have the same rights and duties as you.

C H I   C H I

63

You want to do good things?
Just do them!
Do not expect
recognition, reward and
thanks.
If you do good things
do them because of themselves.
And you will gather
recognition,
reward and
thanks
without noticing it.

If you want to do good things for others then
you should do them without any expectation.
This is the way to avoid disappointment.

䷿ WEI CHI

64

Pureness
does not know where is above
and where is below.
It comes from the void.
To the void it will return.
Pureness
and origin
are one.

You make your own fortune, whatever you undertake. Therefore be responsible, and act in accordance with the higher principle which allows you to live on this earth.

Afterword

Look at
your own life
and know
that your roots,
your trunk,
your branches and your leaves
will live as long
as your character is noble.
Therefore you can be lucky.

About the Author

Chao-Hsiu Chen was born in Taiwan. She learned how to practise yoga and studied music in Vienna and Salzburg. She has studied the teachings of Confucius all her life. Also an expert in the Chinese art of *feng shui*, she has written the books *Chi*, *Feng Shui* and *Body Feng Shui*, all published in Germany. In addition, Chao has published a volume of poetry, *The Buddhist Book of Love*, and is also an artist, having illustrated a number of titles on Chinese and Japanese wisdom, as well as creating the beautiful illustrations featured on the bamboo cards in this pack. She is currently composing theme music for various German television programmes. She speaks five languages and lives in Rome and Munich.

Acknowledgements

EDDISON•SADD EDITIONS

Editorial Director	*Ian Jackson*
Editor	*Tessa Monina*
Proofreader	*Michele Turney*
Art Director	*Elaine Partington*
Mac Designer	*Brazzle Atkins*
Assistant Designer	*Siu Yin Ho*
Production	*Karyn Claridge & Charles James*

Table of Hexagrams

1 CH'IEN (page 14)	2 K'UN (page 16)	3 CHUN (page 18)	4 MENG (page 20)	5 HSU (page 22)	6 SUNG (page 24)	7 SHIH (page 26)	8 PI (page 28)
9 HSIAO CH'U (page 30)	10 LU (page 32)	11 T'AI (page 34)	12 P'I (page 36)	13 T'UNG JEN (page 38)	14 TA YU (page 40)	15 CH'IEN (page 42)	16 YU (page 44)
17 SUI (page 46)	18 KU (page 48)	19 LIN (page 50)	20 KUAN (page 52)	21 SHIH HO (page 54)	22 PI (page 56)	23 PO (page 58)	24 FU (page 60)
25 WU WANG (page 62)	26 TA CH'U (page 64)	27 I (page 66)	28 TA KUO (page 68)	29 K'AN (page 70)	30 LI (page 72)	31 HSIEN (page 74)	32 HENG (page 76)
33 TUN (page 78)	34 TA CHUANG (page 80)	35 CHIN (page 82)	36 MING I (page 84)	37 CHIA JEN (page 86)	38 K'UEI (page 88)	39 CHIEN (page 90)	40 HSIEH (page 92)
41 SUN (page 94)	42 I (page 96)	43 KUAI (page 98)	44 KOU (page 100)	45 TS'UI (page 102)	46 SHENG (page 104)	47 K'UN (page 106)	48 CHING (page 108)
49 KO (page 110)	50 TING (page 112)	51 CHEN (page 114)	52 KEN (page 116)	53 CHIEN (page 118)	54 KUEI MEI (page 120)	55 FENG (page 122)	56 LU (page 124)
57 SUN (page 126)	58 TUI (page 128)	59 HUAN (page 130)	60 CHIEH (page 132)	61 CHUNG FU (page 134)	62 HSIAO KUO (page 136)	63 CHI CHI (page 138)	64 WEI CHI (page 140)